BIBLE STORIES
of Boys and Girls

By Christin Ditchfield

Illustrated by Jerry Smath

🐾 A GOLDEN BOOK • NEW YORK

Copyright © 2010 by Random House, Inc.
All rights reserved.
Published in the United States by Golden Books, an imprint of Random House Children's Books,
a division of Random House, Inc., 1745 Broadway, New York, NY 10019.
Golden Books, A Golden Book, A Little Golden Book, the G colophon, and the distinctive gold
spine are registered trademarks of Random House, Inc.
www.randomhouse.com/kids
Educators and librarians, for a variety of teaching tools, visit us at
www.randomhouse.com/teachers
Library of Congress Control Number: 2008942728
ISBN: 978-0-375-85461-3
Printed in the United States of America
10 9 8 7 6 5 4 3

The Bible is full of stories of boys and girls who did great things for God. They loved Him with all their hearts and learned to walk in His ways.

REBEKAH THE KINDHEARTED

Every evening, Rebekah joined the other girls from her village as they went to the well to draw fresh water for their families. Rebekah had to carry a large pitcher on her shoulder. When it was full, it was very heavy.

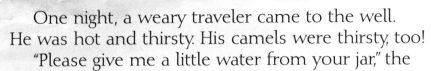

One night, a weary traveler came to the well.
He was hot and thirsty. His camels were thirsty, too!
    "Please give me a little water from your jar," the
traveler said to Rebekah.
    Rebekah gave water to the man and said, "I'll
draw water for your camels, too." It was hard work,
but Rebekah didn't mind.

The traveler was touched by Rebekah's kindness. He had been praying that God would help him find a very special young woman to marry Isaac, his master's son. The master was Abraham, a great man of God.

Now the traveler knew that God had answered his prayers. He asked Rebekah to introduce him to her family. He gave them gifts of gold and silver and fine jewels, for Rebekah had been chosen by God to marry Isaac.

JOSEPH THE DREAMER

Once there was a boy named Joseph. Joseph's father loved him very much. He gave him a gift of a beautiful coat of many colors. This made Joseph's brothers jealous.

God gave Joseph special dreams about things that would happen in the future. Joseph often dreamed that he would do something very important one day, and that his family would be grateful to him.

Joseph's brothers got tired of hearing him
talk about his dreams. They wanted to get rid of
him, so they sold him as a slave. He was taken
far away to Egypt. But God watched over Joseph
as he grew up in that land, because He had a
very special plan for him.

One night, Pharaoh, the king of Egypt, had a frightening dream. With God's help, Joseph told Pharaoh that the dream meant hungry times were coming. Joseph said that the king must start storing up food for his people so that they would have enough to eat for many years.

The king was very pleased with Joseph. "You shall be in charge of my palace and all my people," he told him.

Years later, when Pharaoh's dream came true, there was enough food stored up to feed all the people in the land, and no one went hungry. Now Joseph understood why God had wanted him to live in Egypt. He forgave his brothers for what they had done to him. He even invited them to come and live with him in Egypt so that he could take care of them and their families. They were very grateful—just as he'd dreamed they would be!

MIRIAM THE GOOD SISTER

Many years later, God's people were still living
in Egypt. A new ruler forced them to work as
slaves. He even sent soldiers to harm all the
newborn Hebrew boys. When a baby named
Moses was born, his mother wanted to keep him
safe. She laid him in a basket and hid it among
the reeds by the riverbank.

Moses's older sister, Miriam, was very brave.
Day after day, she stood at the edge of the water,
watching over the baby. She prayed that God
would protect Moses and keep him hidden from
the soldiers.

One day, the king's daughter came to the river
to swim and found the basket with the baby in
it, crying.

"This is one of the Hebrew babies," said the princess. She felt sorry for Moses and decided to keep him. "But someone must care for him," she said.

Miriam came out from her hiding place. "Shall I bring a Hebrew woman to nurse the baby for you?" she asked.

"Yes, go," answered the princess. So Miriam ran and brought her own mother. The princess told her, "Take this baby and nurse him for me, and I will pay you."

The baby Moses would grow up to lead God's people out of slavery in Egypt and back to their homeland. And his sister, Miriam, would be with him every step of the way.

SAMUEL THE PROPHET

Long ago, a woman named Hannah prayed and prayed that God would give her a son. She promised that if He did, she would give the boy back to Him—she would teach her child to love God and serve Him all his life. God answered Hannah's prayers. He gave her Samuel.

When Samuel was still a little boy, his mother took him to live in the temple. There he would learn to serve God.

One night, Samuel heard a voice calling to him. He thought it was Eli, the priest. But when he ran to Eli's room, Samuel found the priest fast asleep. He hadn't called Samuel.

Three times Samuel heard the voice, and three times he ran to Eli. Finally, Eli realized that Samuel was hearing the voice of God.

"The next time you hear the voice," Eli told Samuel, "say, 'Here I am, Lord. I am listening.'"

That night, God spoke to Samuel. He told
Samuel that He wanted him to be His prophet,
His messenger to the people of Israel. All his life,
Samuel would listen to hear God's voice. Whenever
God spoke to him, Samuel would tell the people
everything that God had said. He would teach
them to listen to God, too.

DAVID THE SHEPHERD KING

David was a shepherd boy. His father had put him in charge of watching over the family's sheep. Out in the fields, David learned to play instruments and write songs of praise to God. When danger did come, David called on God for help. God gave him the strength to fight off a lion and a bear to protect his flock of sheep.

One day, David's father asked him to take some food and supplies to his older brothers, who were soldiers in King Saul's army. When David found his brothers, they were shaking with fear. Their enemies had sent a great giant named Goliath to attack them. It made David angry to hear Goliath cursing God and His people.

"I will fight Goliath myself," said David. The giant laughed when he saw the boy coming. But David prayed that God would guide his hands. He put a small stone into his slingshot and hurled it toward Goliath. The stone hit the giant right in the middle of his forehead— and he fell at David's feet.

David grew up to be a brave and mighty warrior. He led the people of Israel into battle against their enemies time and time again. David always asked God to show him what to do. And God was so pleased with David's courage and faith that He made him king.

JESUS, THE SON OF GOD

Jesus was born in Bethlehem, the same city as David. Like David, He would grow up to be a king— the King of Kings.

Even as a child, Jesus was full of God's wisdom. He understood better than anyone how to live a life that pleased God. One day, His mother, Mary, thought she had lost Him. She looked for the little boy everywhere. At last she found Jesus in the Temple, teaching the priests about God's law.

Jesus wanted to help people everywhere grow closer to God and feel His love for them in their hearts.